Call from the Minaret:
A Muslim Family in Britain

Call from the Minaret:
A Muslim Family in Britain

Muhammad Iqbal

Hodder
and Stoughton

Union of Muslim
Organisations

British Library Cataloguing in Publication Data

Iqbal, Muhammad, b. 1938
   Call from the minaret.
   1. Muslims – Great Britain
   I. Title   II. Union of Muslim Organisations
of UK and Eire
   941   DA125.M/
   ISBN 0-340-25682-6

Filmset in Monophoto Plantin
Printed and bound in Great Britain for
Hodder and Stoughton Educational,
a division of Hodder and Stoughton Ltd,
Mill Road, Dunton Green, Sevenoaks, Kent,
by Richard Clay (The Chaucer Press) Ltd, Bungay, Suffolk

Foreword

This is the second book published by the UMO Publications Committee.

It is generally accepted that religion is more deeply ingrained in people of the East than those in the West. The Religion of Islam is unique in the sense that, being the consummation of all revealed religions, it adorns with a touch of modernity all the well-recognized norms of morality and ethics.

To the Western mind, it is unthinkable to conceive of a religion which can furnish principles to govern the conduct of an individual from the cradle to the grave. It is only when practical examples are presented that the reality of Islam as a way of life manifests itself. To that extent, this book *Call from the Minaret: A Muslim Family in Britain* written by Dr Muhammad Iqbal is an excellent contribution. By selecting a Muslim family from Britain as a centrepiece, the author has at the same time attempted to portray the difficulties encountered by a Muslim family in adjusting to the ever-changing environment in this country and at the same time demonstrating the universality and dynamism of the principles of Islam.

By providing a school background on which the various facets of a Muslim's life are projected, this book has the added advantage of furnishing practical and educational knowledge on Islam. The style of the book's presentation is such as to evoke the sympathy and understanding of the readers to the religious beliefs of any Muslim community and in this sense it is a contribution towards better race relations and understanding. Equally, it is a useful link for the Muslim community in Britain with the Muslim world.

Although primarily intended for school children of secondary and upper-junior age groups, it can prove to be interesting for any beginner of Islam. The use of Arabic transliteration, alongside translation, might prove specially attractive to those who are interested in the Arabic language and the text of the essential Muslim prayers.

A series of children's books on Islamic education is also being produced by the UMO Editorial Board with Dr Syed Ali Ashraf as the General Editor.

SYED AZIZ PASHA
General Secretary
Union of Muslim Organizations of UK & Eire
London

November 1979
Dhul Hijja 1399

Acknowledgements

The author wishes to thank the following for their help in planning and writing this book:

Maryam Khanum Iqbal and W. Owen Cole for guidance and encouragement.

Abu Anis Muhammad Barkat Ali, Rector, *Dar-ul-Ehsan*, Faisalabad, Pakistan, for checking facts on Islam.

Information Divisions of the Muslim Embassies in London for photographs and general information.

Huddersfield Community Relations Council for the appendix of Muslim names.

Union of Muslim Organizations of UK and Eire for reproduction of the glossary of Arabic terms and the list of books on Islam from their *Guidelines and Syllabus on Islamic Education.*

Nancy M. Tuke and Jacqueline Hepworth, the Huddersfield Polytechnic, for typing the manuscript.

Dr Syed Ali Ashraf, Professor, King Abdul Aziz University, Jeddah, Saudi Arabia, and Dr Syed Aziz Pasha, General Secretary, Union of Muslim Organizations of UK and Eire for the final perusal of the manuscript.

Hafiz Muhammad Yusuf Sadidi (calligrapher Pakistan Times, Lahore) for the Arabic script.

Many Muslim and British associates for their friendship and a willingness to share their experience.

MUHAMMAD IQBAL

Contents

Our Muslim Family

Bashir Ahmad was born in Pakistan. Like most of the population he is a Muslim. So is his wife Ghulam Fatima.

They now live with their son Muhammad Ajmal and daughter Azra Khanum in a large town, Huddersfield, in the industrial West Riding of Yorkshire.

What brought this family to Great Britain? What are their hopes and fears, their joys and heartaches? How much have they had to learn and adapt their way of life and what have they got to give and teach others?

Let us take a look at what may, until now, have been no more than a coloured patch on a world map. Have a good look at the Punjab, the former home of the Ahmad family and try to imagine the kind of life you might lead in a village in the Punjab. Also, we will attempt to study the background of the other Muslim families who have settled in Great Britain but happen to come from different parts of the Muslim World.

2   *Islam – the Religion*

Both Ahmad's children have settled down well in local schools. When they first arrived they entered a special Reception Centre for newly arrived children who needed education in English as a second language. This not only helped them to speak, read and write English, but helped them to overcome shyness and the initial shock of coming into contact with an entirely new way of life. From this centre they were transferred to a primary school to continue their education in the normal way with class-mates from English, European, West Indian and Asian homes. Naturally, before any real kind of friendship could be formed the children had to have confidence in speaking English. This applies to all children who come to live in Great Britain. Some find it more difficult than others and need to be encouraged not only by their teachers but by their fellow pupils.

Ajmal who is now nine, still attends the junior school where he works and plays quite happily with children of his own age group. For the young pupil, the ability and opportunity to adapt are much easier than for older pupils or adult. His sister Azra is now in her second year at secondary school. She has had to work hard to catch up on all she missed during the vital infant and lower junior stages of education. Her natural desire to learn has helped her to progress and she reads a great deal and takes pride in her work. Her efforts and determination have not gone unnoticed.

Recently her satchel has been heavier than usual. On certain days she brings to school such books as *Muslim Religious Stories*, *The Tales of the Prophets*, *What is Islam?* or even *A*

Brief History of Islam. These are the days of her special religious education lessons. Azra's religious education teacher has prepared a project on Islam this term. He is well aware of the religious needs of Azra and the other Muslim pupils and he knows that their experience can enrich the knowledge and lives of their English class-mates. He has been finding as much as he can about Islam. He hopes the pupils will do the same.

Today's lesson is about Islamic beliefs. Firstly, he explains the meaning of the word Islam. He says it is an Arabic word with two meanings, 'submission to the Will of Allah (personal name for God)' and 'peace'. Therefore a Muslim is a person who submits to the Will of Allah. Azra smiles and nods her head in agreement.

Azra's teacher then tells the class that he is going to ask Azra to answer some particular questions about her religion. She is a little nervous at first, but soon quite forgets about it as her class-mates show such interest in what she is saying. Let's listen to some of the questions . . .

Teacher: What exactly is the religion of Islam?

Azra: My father has explained it to me through a story told by Umar ﴿رضي الله عنه﴾, the Second Caliph of Islam. I have the story here. 'We were all sitting in the company of the Prophet Muhammad (the last Prophet of Islam) when a man dressed in a spotlessly clean white gown came among us. His hair was sparkling black and his face was extremely handsome. He was a stranger to us all. Nobody from Medina (that's in Saudi Arabia), knew him, yet he did not seem to be weary of travelling. We wondered who this could be. He stepped forward and sat close to the Prophet, asking him, "What is Islam?" The Prophet replied, "The belief that no one is worthy of worship but Allah, and Muhammad ﷺ is His Prophet; the saying of **prayers**; payment of *Zakat*; **fasting** in the month of *Ramadhan*; and

the performance of **Pilgrimage**, if savings allow."
The stranger replied, "This is true." We were all
surprised, for the stranger enquired as if he had
not known anything and now he was agreeing with
the answer as if he had known all the time. The
stranger then asked, "What do you believe in?"
The Prophet replied, "Muslims believe in Allah,
the Angels, the revealed books, all the Prophets,
the Day of Resurrection and destiny." The stranger said, "This is also correct." He asked one
more question and the Prophet answered him.
When the man had gone, the Prophet turned to me
and asked, "Do you know who he was?" I said,
"Allah and His Prophet know better." The Prophet said, "He was the Archangel Gabriel who
came to teach you what Islam is.'"

Teacher: And who would you call a Muslim?

Azra: A Muslim is a person who believes with all sin-
cerity in the *Kalimah*.

Teacher: What is that?

Azra: The *Kalimah* is a simple statement —
La ilaha illallah-u Muhammad-ur-Rasool Ullah.
لَا إِلٰهَ إِلَّا اللهُ مُحَمَّدٌ رَّسُوْلُ اللهِ — which means 'No
one is worthy of worship but Allah and Muham-
mad ﷺ is the Messenger of Allah!' We also
believe in *Tauheed* توحِيد — the unity or oneness of
Allah Who is Kind, Merciful, Sustainer, Eternal,
Living, all-Knowing, all-Hearing and all-Seeing.
Allah is best explained in the *Al-Ikhlas* الإخلاص or
Purity the 112th Chapter of the *Holy Quran*.
*Bismillah-ir Rahman-ir Rahim! Qul huwallaho
Ahad Allahussamad. Lam yalid wa lam yulad.
Wa lam yakun lahu kufuwan ahad.*

بِسْمِ اللهِ الرَّحْمٰنِ الرَّحِيْمِ ٥
قُلْ هُوَ اللهُ اَحَدٌ ٥ اَللهُ الصَّمَدُ ٥ لَمْ يَلِدْ هْ وَلَمْ يُوْلَدْ هْ
وَلَمْ يَكُنْ لَّهٗ كُفُوًا اَحَدٌ ٥

4

This means:

In the name of Allah, the Compassionate, the Merciful. Say, 'He is Allah, the One and Only. Allah is eternally besought of all. He does not beget nor was He begotten. And there is none that can be compared with Him.'

Teacher: Azra, you have just mentioned the *Quran*. Isn't that the Holy Book of the Muslims?

Azra: Yes, it is treated with great respect. The Archangel Gabriel first appeared to Muhammad ﷺ in a cave at Hira, then appeared many times in different places over a period of 23 years. The Archangel always brought messages from Allah. The Prophet could neither read nor write but Allah caused them to be retained in his memory once he had heard it and were recorded by his companions whenever it was revealed to him by the Archangel. They, in their turn, learnt the messages. Eventually these verses were written down exactly as they had been told to the Prophet, in the book known as the *Quran*, which means 'recitation'.

Teacher: I will write it on the blackboard as there are two spellings (the first script corresponds to the correct Arabic spelling.)

QURAN   KORAN

Some of us can look for this word in the encyclopaedia afterwards. I have an English translation of the *Holy Quran* here which can be studied later. You say the Archangel Gabriel brought Allah's message to Muhammad ﷺ.

Is it the same Angel mentioned in the *Bible*?

Azra: Oh yes. The *Holy Quran* does recognize the other Holy Scriptures, but mentions only the original Scroll of Prophet Abraham, the *Torah* (Pentateuch, or First 5 books of the Bible) of Prophet

Moses, the Psalms of Prophet David and the *Injeel* of Prophet Jesus (Peace be on them all). The *Holy Quran* mentions that later people added or suppressed many things and the original is therefore lost. The Prophets were sent to all races and tribes in all parts of the world, at different times. Some of them had the Divine Law revealed to them and others just helped to carry it out. Prophets before Muhammad ﷺ like Adam, Abraham, Moses and Jesus (peace be on them all) are specially mentioned. In the Arabic of the *Holy Quran* Jesus is called *Isa* (peace be on him). Muslims believe that Allah has decided what is good and evil, and that He decides our destiny. He has ordered us to do good and resist evil, and that He decides our destiny. Muslims also believe that whatever happens to them is the Will of Allah. An unhappy incident may sadden them and be hard for them to understand, for the true meaning is known to Allah alone.

Teacher: So far we have talked about the *Kalimah* (Belief). This is one of the Five Pillars of Islam. The second is the saying of prayers. Can you tell us something about these?

Azra: Yes, I can. Prayers are acts of worship and are preceded by ablutions, that is washing. There are five calls to prayers each day: the first before sunrise, the next just after mid-day, then in the late afternoon just after the second prayer, after sunset, and finally as twilight disappears. They must be said at the right times. A precise number of *Rak'at*, or units of all the prayers, is accompanied by certain fixed parts of the *Holy Quran* which are recited. The other parts of a unit are chosen by the *Imam*, the leader of the prayers in the Mosque. When we say prayers at home we recite whatever we consider to be appropriate. If you want to see the positions of kneeling, squatting and prostrating which accompany the prayers we could go to the Mosque. The prayers are ended by raising both hands and reciting certain Arabic invocations and then anything else you wish to ask of Allah in Arabic or in any language.

Teacher: Thank you. I think it is a good idea to visit the Mosque. I will see if I can arrange a visit with the Secretary of the Mosque Committee. Could you read something from the *Quran* in Arabic for us?

Azra: I'd be pleased to. This is the first Chapter of the *Holy Quran* called *Al-Fatiha* meaning The Opening. It is always recited in every *Rak'at* of prayer.

Bismillah irrahma – irrahim. Alhamdulillahi Rabbila'lamin. Arrahmanirrahim. Malik-i-Yaumiddin. Iyyaka na'budu wa Iyyakanastain. Ihdinassiratalmustaqim. Siratallazina an'amta ailaihim. Ghairil Maghdubi-alaihim waladdalin. Amin.

بِسْمِ اللهِ الرَّحْمٰنِ الرَّحِيْمِ ٥ اَلْحَمْدُ لِلّٰهِ
رَبِّ الْعٰلَمِيْنَ ٥ الرَّحْمٰنِ الرَّحِيْمِ ٥ مٰلِكِ يَوْمِ الدِّيْنِ ٥
اِيَّاكَ نَعْبُدُ وَ اِيَّاكَ نَسْتَعِيْنُ ٥
اِهْدِنَا الصِّرَاطَ الْمُسْتَقِيْمَ ٥ صِرَاطَ الَّذِيْنَ
اَنْعَمْتَ عَلَيْهِمْ ٥ غَيْرِ الْمَغْضُوْبِ عَلَيْهِمْ
وَلَا الضَّآلِّيْنَ ٥ اٰمِيْنَ ٥

This means:

In the Name of Allah, the Compassionate, the Merciful. Praise be to Allah, the Lord of the Worlds, the Compassionate, the Merciful, the Master of the Day of Judgement. You alone we worship and You alone we ask for help. Show us the straight path: the path of those whom You have favoured; not of those who earn Your anger, nor of those who go astray. *Amin.*

Teacher: Well done. *Salat* then, the saying of prayers, is

7

the second Pillar of Islam. Which is the third?

Azra: Fasting for the full lunar month of *Ramadhan*. This means that we must not eat, drink, smoke, make love or entertain ourselves in any way from dawn until sunset. We gain a great deal from this fasting. The spirit is strengthened by the weakening of the body; the habits of self-control, submissiveness and self-discipline are developed and we feel closer to Allah.

Teacher: *Zakat* is the fourth Pillar. One fortieth or two and a half per cent of a person's yearly savings in cash and kind are given to the poor or any charity that Islamic law allows. So a man who saves £100 a year would be required to give away £2·50 of it. I wonder if Azra would tell us why the *Hajj* (Pilgrimage) is important, for this is the fifth Pillar of Islam.

Azra: When Hajera (Hagar), the wife of the Prophet Abraham gave birth to a son, Ishmael, Allah ordered the Prophet to leave them both in a deserted and infertile valley. Hajera rested the baby under the shade of a stone and went in search of water; she could not find any. The thirsty baby began kicking his heels when suddenly water gushed from the earth under his feet. This was by the will of Allah; today the fountain is known as *Zam-Zam*. Seeing this, an Arab tribe settled there and the city of Mecca grew up. Later on, Prophet Abraham and his son Prophet Ishmael rebuilt the cube-shaped structure originally built by the Prophet Adam (Peace be on them all). This structure came to be known as the *Kaaba*, a plce of worship and pilgrimage for many people in Arabia and the Muslim World. When Ishmael was a young boy, Allah came to Prophet Abraham in a dream and told him to sacrifice his son. The Prophet was a true lover of Allah. He did as he was commanded and set off to make the sacrifice, having told his son what Allah had asked him to do. The Devil, Satan, tried to stop them but the Prophet and his son Ishmael became angry and threw small stones at him. Soon they came to Mina, a place nearby. He tied his son's hands and feet together and put a bandage over his own eyes so that he could not see what he was about to do. Before he could strike his son's throat with his knife, he heard a Divine voice saying 'You have fulfilled what you saw (in your dream). Allah has given you instead a momentous sacrifice.' When the Prophet took the blindfold from his eyes he saw a ram running down the hill. He and Ishmael caught the ram and sacrificed it.

Teacher: It would be interesting to compare this with the Old Testament story. Yes, do continue Azra.

Azra: Every year, on the 10th of *Dhu-al-Hijjah* (the 12th Month of the Muslim year), Muslims who can afford it, travel to Mecca and sacrifice a lamb, goat or sheep to commemorate the sacrifice of Prophet Ishmael at Mina, and this is the day of Eid-al-Adha – a day of great rejoicing especially for the children.

Teacher: Thank you very much for being so helpful, Azra. You have given us a lot to think and talk about. Next we will find out all we can about the Muslim place of worship, the Mosque, and the life story of the Prophet Muhammad صلى الله عليه وسلم peace be upon him.

3 Muhammad ﷺ, the Prophet

From time to time Allah the Almighty sent prophets for the correct guidance of the people. They were innumerable, so much so that at one time there was scarcely a place which did not have its own prophet. Sometimes their work was received kindly and sometimes they and their followers were persecuted to such an extent that Allah punished the unbelievers. Some of the prophets mentioned in the *Holy Quran* are Adam, Noah, Abraham, Lot, Joseph, Shoaib, Moses, David, Solomon, Jonah and Jesus (Peace be on them all). They all professed submission to the Will of Allah the Almighty and desired peace on earth. This is, in fact, the belief of Islam.

Muhammad ﷺ is the last Prophet about whom it is made perfectly clear from the *Quranic* verses which Allah the Almighty has revealed to us thus:

'We sent you not but as a Mercy for all creatures'.
— (*Al-Qur'an — Chapter 21, verse 107*)

Muhammad ﷺ is a unique person in the history of mankind.

This then is the basic belief of all true Muslims who know from the collection of the *Hadith* that just as Allah the Almighty exists everywhere, Muhammad's ﷺ kindness is attendant also. As Muhammad ﷺ was a perfect personification of the human being with angelic qualities and the sole authority of the True Knowledge of the Attributes of Allah the Almighty, to copy his way of life, called *Ittiba'* in juridical terms, will prove the redemption of one's soul and profitable in the life here and Hereafter.

As a descendant of Prophet Ishmael, Muhammad ﷺ was born on the morning of *22 April, 571 CE* to Abdullah, the son of Abdul Mutalib, the head of the Quraish tribe in Mecca. His father had died before his birth and he lost his mother at the age of 6. He was taken into the care of his grandfather who died when Muhammad ﷺ was eight. Abu Talib, his uncle and father of Ali ﵁ the Fourth Caliph of Islam, then took charge of the orphan.

Even before being invested with Prophethood, Muhammad ﷺ had no interest in deities. The people of those days were nomads, multi-idolatrous, barbarous, immoral, vain and female infant murderers. They had their own peculiar habits of hospitality, heroism and self-respect. Muhammad ﷺ was meditative and withdrawn from all this, but he was often called to settle disputes because of his renowned honesty, righteousness and truthfulness. He was now known as Al-Amin (the trusted one).

When Muhammad ﷺ grew up he worked as a tradesman for a wealthy Meccan widow who, at the age of forty, proposed that they should marry because she found him such an honest and diligent person. Muhammad ﷺ who was only twenty-five at that time agreed to the proposal. Later on Muhammad ﷺ began to visit a cave in a hill near Mecca called Hira, where he meditated regularly, until the age of forty, when he received a Divine Call (*Al-Qur'an* 96:1–5).

As instructed by Allah, he began to spread his Faith among his near and dear ones and then among the Meccans. He was persecuted by the Meccan unbelievers. But gradually some people who had previously ridiculed and jeered at his words began to follow him seriously as more and more people embraced Islam. His uncles Abu Lahab and Abu Jahl from the Quraish tribe were annoyed by Muhammad's ﷺ teaching and success.

Once Abu Bakr رضي الله عنه rescued him from near strangulation. The throwing of dust and dirt were quite common incidents to show hatred for the Prophet. His uncle Abu Talib was his protector. The unbelievers asked him to stop Muhammad صلى الله عليه وسلم from preaching about the worship of one Allah instead of many, but Abu Talib who had reared him was so concerned about his safety that he offered his protection though he never accepted Islam in his life time.

As time passed, some Muslim families migrated to Abyssinia. Hamza and Umar, the notable chiefs of the Quraish tribe, also accepted Islam. When oppression failed to oust Islam, social boycott followed and they were forced to camp in an infertile valley Shib Abi Talib where the death rate rose rapidly. They were, eventually, allowed to return to Mecca with the hope that leniency might sever their bonds with Islam but this was not fulfilled.

In the tenth year of his preaching, his uncle and wife died. In the next two years seventy-two pilgrims from Medina accepted Islam and pledged his safety and protection in case of their migration. Muhammad صلى الله عليه وسلم sent in groups those of his followers who wanted to migrate. At last he and Abu Bakr رضي الله عنه left at the command of Allah and the Meccans took up the chase. Abu Bakr رضي الله عنه and the Prophet remained in a Cave in Mount Saur for three days. When the search was over they reached Medina on the *8th Rabi-al-Awwal* (16 July, 622 CE).

The Muslims were threatened even in Medina by the Quraish of Mecca and in the second year of emigration a famous battle between 313 ill-equipped Muslims and 1,000 well-prepared and mounted warriors from Mecca took place at Badar in the outskirts of Medina. The enemy sustained heavy losses of life and armour. A year later, three thousand soldiers with experienced generals like Khalid bin Walid, were stationed on the outskirts of Medina at the foot of Mount Uhud. To meet the attack Muhammad صلى الله عليه وسلم led 700 men while 300 men were led by Abdullah bin Ubayy who betrayed the Muslims by conspiring with the Meccans.

Muhammad ﷺ had sent men to guard the nearby pass in order to avoid attack from the rear. The enemy discovered this fact and attacked them, following this up with a rapid attack on the main section. Rumours that Muhammad ﷺ had been killed spread throughout the ranks. The Muslims became disheartened, lost many men and the enemy won a partial victory. Muhammad ﷺ lost a tooth. A lady who lost her father, brother and husband in the battle is said to have heaved a sigh of relief when she heard that Muhammad ﷺ was safe. They all loved their illustrious leader.

In the 5th AH, the Battle of Uhud was followed by the battle of the Trench, when the beseiged Muslims were attacked by thousands of unbelievers. A strong wind blew their tents away during the night and the seige was over. No more battles followed except for those started by Jews who were indignant at Muhammad's ﷺ rise to power. There were constant threats upon his life.

In the 6th AH (Muslim calendar year), such events as the annual pilgrimage by Muhammad ﷺ and his followers went to Mecca to perform *Hajj* but they were not allowed to enter Mecca. The unbelievers, however, signed the Treaty of Hudaibiya and there was some peace. In the following year 2,000 people went to Mecca for *Hajj*, without any fears. Muhammad ﷺ now despatched his message to the rulers of the Roman and the Persian emperors inviting them to accept Islam as the only true religion. They did not do so. On the other hand they attacked the Muslims and thus the fight between the Muslims and the Roman and Persian empires started. The Treaty of Hudaibiya had now been terminated because of the violation of its terms by the Meccans. A large number of Muslims marched to and camped outside Mecca. The message to submit was sent and they did so apart from a few who offered up some resistance. The *Kaaba*, the oldest sanctuary of the world, came into the hands of the Muslims. A nomad tribe of Hawazin gathered round the outskirts of Mecca and a decisive battle was fought and won by the Muslims. No person was forced to change his religion. All offenders were pardoned and the war booty was shared by all. The Prophet Muhammad ﷺ himself returned to Medina and made his journey to it on the *8th Dhu-al-Qidah 8 AH*.

People came to see him from far and wide. He lived a simple life, milking his own goats, massaging his camel, cleaning his own shoes and sleeping on a coarse bed. He received everyone regardless of wealth, and discussed all matters. Tolerant and forbearing, he allowed visiting Christians to perform their rites in his Mosque, which later on came to be known as *Masjid-al-Nabvi* (The Prophet's Mosque). However, he specifically asked pagan converts to smash their idols. Mecca became the focal point for everyone.

In the *10th AH*, he delivered his famous sermon to 120,000 people in the Valley of Arafat where he discharged the final rites of his *Hajj* (See *Hujja't-ul-Wida' – The Farewell Pilgrimage*, Barkat Ali; Dar-ul-Ehsan Publications for further details). But the following year in the month of *Safar-ul-Muzaffar* he became afflicted by a fatal fever. He died on the *12th Rabi-al-Awwal*, performing his religious duties to the last. His tomb in the *Masjid-al-Nabvi* is visited annually by millions of people from all parts of the world and is a source of blessing for the whole mankind. His own life history is preserved in his *Hadith*. His sons Ibrahim and Qasim died in infancy and no male issue was left. All those who claim to be his descendants are through his grandsons Imam Hasan and Imam Husain, may Allah the Almighty be pleased with them.

4   *The Mosque*

In Mecca there stands a large cube-shaped building covering sixty square feet of land. It is called the *Kaaba*. Of all the sanctuaries of the world, this is regarded by the Muslims as the first Mosque, or house of Allah, and occupies a unique position among Mosques because of its historical and spiritual significance. The Prophet Adam is supposed to have constructed the *Kaaba*, and the Prophet Abraham with the assistance of his son Prophet Ishmael (Peace be on them all) are reported to have rebuilt it. The Prophet Muhammad ﷺ purified it from idols. Wherever and whenever Muslims pray they always face the direction of the *Kaaba*. In the eastern corner of the *Kaaba* is a small black stone, the *Hajr-e-Aswad*. During the repairing of the *Kaaba* a dispute arose as to which Arab chieftain should have the honour of replacing the Black Stone. So great was the rivalry that they were ready to fight over the matter until Abu Umayya, an elder of the Quraish tribe, suggested that they should ask the advice of the first man to enter the Mosque in the morning. That man was the Prophet Muhammad ﷺ respected by all the tribal chiefs. They agreed to accept his decision. The Prophet ﷺ asked for a cloak to be laid on the ground; on this was placed the stone. He then asked the four chieftains to hold the corners of the cloak and lift the stone. The Prophet ﷺ himself picked up the stone and placed it on the wall. The rebuilding work continued without any blood having been shed.

The Prophet and his companions played a great part in building the Mosque in Medina (Saudi Arabia). It is known

15

as *Masjid-al-Nabvi*, and is held in high esteem by Muslims. *Masjid* is the Arabic word for 'Mosque' and literally means 'a place of prostration'.

The architectural plan for the *Masjid-al-Nabvi* became a model for future Mosques. Murals and floral designs were derived from the Arabic scripts in the *Holy Quran* and minarets, big tombs, radiant halls, pearl-embedded pillars, elevated seats and measured arches became prominent and often exquisitely decorated features of Muslim architecture. One of the most famous pieces of Muslim architecture, the Taj Mahal, is still regarded as a magnificent work of art. Built for the Emperor of India, Shah Jahan, in memory of his wife Mumtaz Mahal, this building consists of two parts, a tomb and a Mosque. The Mosque, situated on the West side of the tomb (on the bank of the river Jamana) so that Muslims do not face the tomb while praying. The Muslim inhabitants of cities like Cairo (Egypt), Qartaba (Spain), Sofia (Bulgaria), Baghdad (Iraq), Istanbul (Turkey), Delhi (India), Lahore (Pakistan) and Damascus (Syria), built elaborate Mosques, to bring beauty into their lives. The natural beauty of the deserts in the Middle East were enhanced by simple architectural construction.

In Islam, idols, statues and people must not be worshipped; Muslims may only pray to Allah. So the Muslim artists and architects have never displayed their affection and respect for their great religious leaders in the form of portraits and busts, although there was a period when the Muslim conquerors of the territories in India, Persia, Spain and Morocco used their leisure time to make portraits which appeared on mugs, arches and in books. The *Safvid* Caliphate of Persia, especially Shah Abbas in the early seventeenth century, took a great deal of interest in the decorations of tombs and Mosques in Isfahan and Shiraz, with glazed tiles, floral designs and murals.

Tourist resorts, gardens and places for public officials

were built. The decorations included circular, rhombic and poly-shaped tombs, figurative drawings and flower petals engraved in stone accompanied by writings from the *Holy Quran*.

It is through these writings that Muslims have excelled in the art of calligraphy (beautiful writing) and have developed a fine and free Arabic hand-writing. There are two styles, *Kufic* round and bold letters and *Nasakh*, long and cursive letters. The former dates back to the time of the Prophet Muhammad ﷺ. This style was later replaced by the *Nasakh* style, which has developed over the years to appear in paintings by Muslims and European artists.

Arnold in *Painting in Islam* quotes an Arab writer and painter as saying, 'The art of writing is an honourable and soul-nourishing accomplishment; as a manual attainment it is always elegant and enjoys general approval.' Imagine its honour and importance when Allah Himself says in the *Holy Quran*:

'Read in the name of thy Lord Who creates man from a clot. Read, and your Lord is the most bounteous Who teaches by the pen; teaches man that he knew not (96:1–5)' and 'even all the trees in the earth were pens and the sea with seven more seas to help it were ink, the word of Allah could not be exhausted. So Allah is mighty Wise (31:2).'

When Allah swears by the pen and what it writes the Muslim cannot help but love the art of calligraphy. The Prophet's disapproval of the drawing of profiles and engraving busts has also enhanced its development.

In Britain there are several purpose-built Mosques, like the one at Woking and one at Manchester, which are of customary design. Similar Mosques have been built at London and Birmingham. The contributions for the construction of these huge buildings are received not only from the Muslims in the United Kingdom, but from Muslims all over the world. Near where Ahmad lives in Huddersfield, an old terraced house has been turned into a Mosque, as has been done in many other English towns.

Having left the Punjab, Ahmad tries very hard to help his family maintain the religious practices which were once part of their daily lives. Of course, he is faced with problems. His children return from school singing Christian hymns to Prophet Jesus. To the Muslim, Jesus is a Prophet as Muhammad ﷺ was, and no Muslim would think of worshipping Muhammad ﷺ. They are also full of delight at the thoughts of Merry Christmas. Ahmad is shocked to hear the Muslim *Eid* (times of rejoicing) referred to as 'our Christmas' by his children. He knows it is more important than ever that the children are given extra lessons about Islam at home and at the Mosque if they are to understand their religion at all. But what young child would not prefer to watch television or play with his friends rather than sit down to more learning after a day at school? No longer does the child see the familiar domes and minarets. Church bells replace the *Adhan*, the Call to Prayers, five times every day. It all seems so far away now! The male Muslim is required to go to a Mosque for worship, though prayers can be said almost anywhere. In Huddersfield, as in other English towns and cities, whenever Muslims pray they face the *Kaaba* in Mecca. The position is specified.

Ahmad says his mid-day prayers at work and one or two at the Mosque in the evening. The sermon is delivered in Arabic (the language of the *Holy Quran*) and translated into English. The *Imam* (the religious leader) at the Huddersfield Mosque is addressed as *Hafiz* if he knows the *Holy Quran* by heart. He welcomes the worshippers to the Mosque.

The *Imam's* job is not only to lead Muslims in prayer, but to teach and set an example of goodness. There is no hierarchy of priesthood in Islam such as that found in the Christian church. The Imam owes his allegiance to Allah and to his community and his family.

Non-Muslims who visit the Mosque are often surprised

not to see pictures of human beings such as Prophets or Great Leaders of Islam hanging on the walls. Instead pictures of the *Kaaba* and Arabic prayers with Urdu or English translations adorn the rooms. The *Minbar*, a raised dais where the *Imam* sits, occupies a central position at the front of the main prayer room. A monthly timetable of the times of prayers hangs on the wall and copies of this are available for those who wish to say prayers regularly. The large prayer hall of the Mosque is fully carpeted but no furniture is kept there.

The large Friday afternoon prayers give you some idea of how Muslims pray. First of all the *Adhan*, which is described below, is recited.

The Adhan

Allah-u-akbar; Allah-u-akbar; Allah-u-akbar; Allah-u-akbar. Ashhaduan la ilaha illallah; Ashhaduan la ilaha illallah, Ashhadu anna Muhammader – Rasulullah, Ashhaduanna Muhammader – Rasulullah. Hayya – alassalah Hayya – alassalah. Hayya – Alalfalah Hayya – alalfalah. Allah-u-akbar Allah-u-akbar. La ilaha illallah.

اَللهُ اَكْبَرُ ٥ اَللهُ اَكْبَرُ ٥ اَللهُ اَكْبَرُ ٥ اَللهُ اَكْبَرُ ٥
اَللهُ اَكْبَرُ ٥
اَشْهَدُ اَنْ لَّا اِلٰهَ اِلَّا اللهُ ٥ اَشْهَدُ اَنْ
لَّا اِلٰهَ اِلَّا اللهُ ٥ اَشْهَدُ اَنَّ مُحَمَّدًا
رَّسُوْلُ اللهِ ٥ اَشْهَدُ اَنَّ مُحَمَّدًا
رَّسُوْلُ اللهِ ٥ حَيَّ عَلَى الصَّلٰوةِ ٥ حَيَّ
عَلَى الصَّلٰوةِ ٥ حَيَّ عَلَى الْفَلَاحِ ٥
حَيَّ عَلَى الْفَلَاحِ ٥ اَللهُ اَكْبَرُ ٥ اَللهُ اَكْبَرُ ٥
لَّا اِلٰهَ اِلَّا اللهُ ٥

Allah is great; Allah is great; Allah is great; Allah is great. I bear witness that no one is worthy of worship except Allah. I bear witness that no one is worthy of worship except Allah. I also bear witness that Muhammad is the Messenger of Allah. I also bear witness that Muhammad is the Messenger of Allah. O brethren in Islam! Come to perform the prayers. O brethren in Islam! Come to perform the prayers. O brethren in Islam! Come to achieve salvation. O brethren in Islam! Come to achieve salvation. Allah is great; Allah is great. No one is worthy of worship except Allah.

Before entering the prayer hall to worship, people perform ablution known as *Wudhu*. They wash their hands up to the wrists, rinse the mouth, run water through the nostrils, wash the face including ears, forehead and chin, the arms beyond elbows. This is followed by the rubbing of the head and ears with wet fingers, and finally the right foot and left foot are cleaned up to the ankles. *Bismillah* (In the name of Allah) is recited at the beginning and other formulas are recited during the ablutions. The people say four units, or two units, of prayers (*Rak'at*) individually. The *Imam* comes in unobtrusively, says his *Sunnah* prayers, and leads the assembled Muslims in congregational *Fard* prayers. On Friday afternoon for example, he explains the significance of *Eid-al-Adha* and the two Eid prayers (described previously) and the various customs which the pilgrims at Mecca perform during pilgrimage on the eve of this Eid. He delivers a sermon on a chosen subject, this is usually his address at the beginning of the month (in the Muslim Calendar) *Dhu-al-Hijjah*.

When the time for the *Jamaat* (congregational prayers) approaches, a man stands up and says the *Adhan*, and then the *Imam* reads the *Khutba* (sermon). Traditionally it is in Arabic which only a few non-Arabic speaking Muslims are able to understand fully and comprises theological and practical subjects as well as blessings to the Prophet Muhammad ﷺ and his companions. At the end of the *Khutba* the religious leader stands in front facing the direction of the *Kaaba* in Mecca, with the people in rows behind him. He recites small portions from the *Holy Quran* and gives the commands, 'Allah-u-*Akbar*' (Allah is Great). At this, everybody kneels, then stands upright. At a series of commands they prostrate, sit, prostrate again and stand up. All this is repeated after another recitation from the *Holy Quran*, but they all sit and recite quietly. They pray to Allah for the forgiveness of their sins and strength to do good to others which is also the main point of the prayer units. After congregational prayers, people say some more prayer units (*Sunnah*) privately to themselves and leave.

One aspect of life at the Mosque which differs from that in other churches of different faiths is the fact that men and women do not congregate together in the same place although they say prayers at the same Mosque. Indeed, it is considered to be very important that the mother of the family prays regularly and helps her children to lead the life of a good Muslim. Most women stay at home to pray but there is another room available for them in the Mosque. Muslims believe that while saying prayers a person's whole attention must be upon Allah. This segregation of men from women during the saying of prayers often appears to non-Muslims to be odd and unfair. It is not so – there is more chance of keeping one's attention upon prayer and not allowing the mind to wander, if they pray separately.

Attached to the Mosque is a Community Centre, which caters for the cultural, educational and social life of both adults and children. Ahmad and his fellow Muslims have contributed towards the cost of a new Community Centre building which now takes up the former back-garden of the old house. Here, meetings are held and sporting activities for all age groups of children are arranged.

5   *Azra and Ajmal at the Mosque*

Today, Mosques all over the world are still used, in addition to the saying of congregational prayers, for important teaching, discourses and lectures for the promotion of Islam. There are annexes to the main building which are used as schools where children are taught Islamic faith and theology.

In English schools there are no fixed arrangements for children to learn about Islam and the Muslim way of life, except in a few areas where qualified Muslim teachers visit the schools just before or after school hours for this purpose. The Mosque, however, does have a certain role and the religious leader has specific duties to perform. This is why Azra and Ajmal visit the local Mosque in the evening, on week-days and during the day over the week-ends for one-hourly lessons. These lessons take up three to five hours per week. Some children do not attend classes at all while others spend ten to twelve hours per week in Islamic studies. During the lessons the children are taught the Urdu and Arabic languages and to read the *Holy Quran* with as much understanding as possible.

Azra has some knowledge of Urdu from her early education at a school in Pakistan. She does not find it as difficult to read the *Holy Quran* as Ajmal does. The Urdu and Arabic alphabets are the same except that a few letters are missing in the latter. Both are written and read from right to left. The Urdu language is a mixture of many different languages and derives words from almost all the North Indian languages and dialects such as Hindi, Punjabi, Gujrati, Marathi and Bengali but a large number of words are of Persian and Arabic origin.

Look at the Urdu Alphabet. It consists of 36 letters made up of both consonants and near-consonants with approximately ten near-vowels. Once the sounds of the Urdu letters are learnt, the reading of the *Holy Quran* in Arabic is made much easier. Let us join Azra and Ajmal with their friends. They are sitting in the school room at the Mosque. They have their own books and are reading to themselves while the *Imam* attends to each child individually. Today Ajmal, wearing his skull cap, recites his prepared passage from the *Holy Quran*. He already knows quite a few *suras* or chapters. Azra is finding out about the Prophets. The Imam has given her a book of stories and a particular history book so that she may further her knowledge.

As Ajmal repeats his new passage of scripture he wonders whether he will ever be able to learn it all. He looks at his little book. It is not the whole of the *Holy Quran* as it is divided into thirty equal-sized volumes which make it easier to carry to and from the Mosque. He looks at all the books stacked on the high shelves. There is a number of copies of the *Holy Quran*; 'How many chapters are there?' he asks the Imam.

'114 chapters, each divided into verses. The long chapters are at the beginning and the shorter at the end' is the reply.

'Those books look very old,' Ajmal continues.

'Yes, they are and we must handle them with great care and respect,' the Imam points out. 'One of the seven copies compiled by Uthman ﷺ, the Third Caliph of Islam in CE 623, is still kept at the Tashkent Museum in Russia. All our modern copies of the *Holy Quran* are based upon it. We must always keep our copy of the *Holy Quran* clean and wrapped up if possible and remember not to turn our backs on it. Now, children, who can tell me what we call people who chant the beautiful rhythmic poetry of the *Holy Quran?*' Everyone begins to look puzzled until Akram calls out, '*Qaris*'. 'That's right,' the *Imam* confirms. 'At the end of the year we'll have a little competition where you can each recite some of the verses you have learnt. Well, Ajmal, I can see you have been doing your homework. I would like you to learn the next two verses for the next lesson. Azra will be able to help you.'

Besides the continual study of the *Holy Quran*, Azra and Ajmal have memorized the contents of *salat* or prayer and how it is to be performed. The five prayers performed during the day are known as *Fajr, Zuhr, Asr, Maghrib* and *Isha*. They are all different and follow a definite pattern of their own. Each session is timed by a 'Call to Prayer' by a *Muezzin* and may last from five to twenty minutes.

In addition to teaching the children, conducting prayers and looking after the Mosque, the *Imam* is called upon to conduct marriage, *aqiqa* (or naming) ceremonies and funeral prayers as and when the occasion arises. Being a Hafiz himself, the *Imam* at the Huddersfield Mosque lays great stress on the respect owed to the *Holy Quran*, as a complete guide to the Muslim's social, cultural, political and spiritual life.

Practical Suggestions

Try to build up a collection of pictures and photographs of famous Mosques and examples of Muslim architecture from all over the world. Help can be sought from local libraries, Muslim Embassies in London or such magazines as *Geography* and *Photography*. The filmstrip *East Comes West* (Yorkshire Committee for Community Relations – Leeds) could be shown.

Study the designs and pattern formations on the walls of Mosques. Pick out the most attractive and copy them – make your own prints and produce original designs based upon the ideas gained from the pictures. Collect samples of Arabic writing and floral designs for a carpet. Design a prayer mat.

Charity – Children could work out some problems based on the Zakat percentage. Consider why charity is one of the five pillars of Islam and find out why it was so essential in the time of the Prophet Muhammad ﷺ. Does it apply as well today?

Try to imagine what it is like to fast from dawn to sunset – how would you feel at first, what are the mental and physical effects? In which ways does modern Western civilization make fasting easier or more difficult than in the time of the Prophet Muhammad ﷺ? Can it teach modern man anything?

Discuss the idea of Pilgrimage – find out about other pilgrimages throughout history and their significance – what do Muslims gain from the *Hajj*? (See also the chapter on Islamic Brotherhood.) Make a tape recording of parts of the prayers recited by a young Muslim.

The following is the translation of an Urdu poem entitled *A Child's Prayer* which is sung in the morning assembly in the schools throughout Pakistan.

My desire to be a light-emanating lamp finds its expression in my prayers, O Lord, let my life be a lamp.

25

And let the darkness of ignorance for ever be foreign to my mind's
*   firmament.*
O Lord, let me be enfolded eternally by light.
Just as the garden wears its crown of flowers, so let my country
*   uphold me with pride.*
Let me, my Lord, be in flower for ever and ever more.
An insatiable thirst for knowledge be mine,
O Lord, give me the passion to pursue the Light of knowledge to
*   the end like the flickering fireflies.*
Let my life be a dedication to the cause of the poor, old and sick.
O Lord, let me always be kind, loving and friendly to all.
And above all, keep me for ever away from the bourne of evil
*   thoughts,*
And guide me, Lord, always along the path pure and right.

Make a collection of similar poems and prayers and use them in an assembly. Children may like to write their own prayers. Some Muslim religious stories equivalent to Biblical stories on love and care may be narrated and acted to create active interest in Islamic civilization and reveal links between Islam and Christianity.

6 *Festivals Round the Year*

The teacher knows that Azra has been fasting for some time. But now she tells him that she will be away from school for a day because the Ahmad family is celebrating *Eid-ul-Fitr* which marks the end of *Ramadhan* – a day of feasting and rejoicing; giving and receiving gifts, new clothes and *Eidi* or cash money. 'This, like other Muslim festivals is subject to the lunar calendar', the teacher explains to Azra's classmates. The lunar calendar began on July 16 CE 622 marking the first of *Muharram*, the month which started the year in which the Prophet Muhammad ﷺ migrated from Mecca to Medina, and consists of twelve months:

Months	Festivals during the Month
1. *Muharram*	10th. Anniversary of the martyrdom of Imam Hussain the grandson of the Prophet Muhammad ﷺ.
2. *Safar*	
3. *Rabi-al-Awwal*	8th. *Hijrah* the migration of the Prophet Muhammad ﷺ from Mecca to Medina. 12th. *Milad-un-Nabi*, the Prophet Muhammad's ﷺ Birthday.
4. *Rabi-al-Thani*	
5. *Jamadi-al-Awwal*	
6. *Jamadi-al-Thani*	
7. *Rajjab*	27th. *Shab-e-Miraj*, Prophet Muhammad's ﷺ Ascension to Heaven (through Jerusalem).

27

8. *Sha'ban*	15th. *Shal-e-Barat.* Night of blessing when the fates of people are decided.
9. *Ramadhan*	The month of fasting. 27th. *Leilat-al-Qadar,* The Night of Power.
10. *Shawal*	1st. *Eid-al-Fitr.*
11. *Dhu-al-Qidah*	
12. *Dhu-al-Hijjah*	9th. The day of *Hajj,* i.e. of Pilgrimage. 10th. *Eid-ul-Adha.*

The 1st, 7th, 11th and 12th months are specifically mentioned in the *Holy Quran* as sacred. The prayers to Allah during these months are met with great joy and kindness by Him. The 10th of *Muharram* is called *Ashoura* and also marks the martyrdom of Imam Hussain, the Prophet Muhammad's ﷺ grandson who fought against the evil forces of the day. It is recommended that Muslims observe an optional fast on this day.

The next important date in the calendar is the 12th *Rabi-al-Awwal,* that is *Milad-un-Nabi,* the Prophet's Birthday which is also the day when the Prophet died. Besides popular celebrations, special lectures and remembrances are arranged. In the early days of Islam, little attention was paid to this event but it is gaining more appeal because of the uniqueness of the message the Prophet brought to mankind.

The Muslims are commanded to observe fasting in the month of *Ramadhan,* the successful completion of which is marked by the happiest day in a Muslim's life, *Eid-al-Fitr,* which is celebrated on the 1st *Shawal. Eid-al-Fitr* is also the day of special congregational prayers marking the end of *Ramadhan.* According to the Prophet's tradition no work must be done on this day. The festival of *Eid-al-Adha* is celebrated on the 10th *Dhu-al-Hijjah.* It commemorates the near sacrifice of Prophet Ishmael, Prophet Abraham's son.

28

An animal (sheep, cow or camel) is sacrificed, prayers are said, and general rejoicing (as for *Eid-al-Fitr*) is celebrated.

Some other festivals of importance are *Shab-e-Miraj*, which celebrates the Prophet Muhammad's ﷺ Ascension to Heaven, *Shab-e-Barat*, when the fates of the people are decided, and *Leilat-al-Qadar*, a Night of Power, which occurs in the third part of *Ramadhan*, most probably on the 27th day, and reminds Muslims of the beginning of the *Quranic* revelations in that month. Many prayers are said and great hospitality is shown, towards relatives, friends and the poor, on the eve of these festivals.

Some children still remember that a few years ago *Eid-al-Fitr* was celebrated a couple of days before Christmas. The teacher reminds the children that the lunar year is ten to eleven days shorter than the solar year. He gives the children the following chart:

Christian Era	Hijrah Year	1st Muharram	Prophet's Day	1st Ramadhan	Eid-al-Adha
1979–	1399	2 Dec '78	10 Feb '79	26 July '79	1 Nov '79
1980–	1400	22 Nov '79	31 Jan '80	15 July '80	21 Oct '80
1981–	1401	9 Nov '80	20 Jan '81	4 July '81	9 Oct '81
1982–	1402	31 Oct '81	9 Jan '82	24 June '82	30 Sept '82
1983–	1403	20 Oct '82	29 Dec '82	13 June '83	20 Sept '83
1984–	1404	9 Oct '83	18 Dec '83	2 June '84	9 Sept '84
1985–	1405	28 Sept '84	12 Dec '84	22 May '85	29 Aug '85

A difference of one day on either side of the dates given above can be taken into account subject to the sighting of the new moon. All Muslim festivals are subject to the phases of the moon. In England low clouds might obscure the moon altogether and delay the start of the festival. So the religious leaders confirm the time by telephoning religious institutions in Muslim countries where there is more likelihood of the moon being sighted in clear skies. The teacher has prepared this chart with the help from the HM Nautical Almanac Office, Royal Greenwich Observatory, which already co-operated with the Islamic Cultural Centre in London to compile a timetable which gives the times for the Muslim daily prayers in London in an average year until the end of the century. The timetable is issued free and can be amended according to the situation of the various places.

Back at school Azra tells her class-mates and the teacher what happened on the *Eid*-day. Many people send *Eid* cards containing greetings and good wishes. These are often scented or highly decorative, showing pictures of famous Mosques, new moon, flowers or Arabic versions from the *Holy Quran*. She is now looking forward to the communal party which the Muslim Association has planned for the week-end. The gathering is usually held on the *Eid-al-Fitr* itself but in England this is not yet recognized as a holiday but Muslim workers take a day off for celebrations at home. Azra hands her teacher an invitation and informs him that they hope to see many other friends from the English community including teachers, social workers, local authority officials and many more. The men provide the entertainment while the women prepare special dishes at home, ready for the party.

7   *Muslim Ceremonies*

A Wedding

Fatima is very proud of her wedding photographs which she shows to her Home Tutor. As she becomes more interested Fatima tells her about some marriage customs in Pakistan.

A daughter is traditionally regarded as a guest in the house, to be cherished and nurtured until the time of her marriage. Choosing a husband for her is regarded as her parents' responsibility but they also consider her wishes. The parents feel relieved only after they have fulfilled their great responsibility and given her away in marriage. The wedding ceremony is therefore the fulfilment of the hope and dreams of not only the bridal pair but the whole family.

All marriage ceremonies are designed to symbolize future bliss and fertility for the wedded couple. Customarily, the friends of the bride praise her and make fun of the groom. He is teased and made to realize that it is not easy to take away a cherished daughter.

The young couple are given presents by their friends and relatives. Gifts are also exchanged between the parents and near relatives of the bridal pair. A set of clothes is a traditional gift. This is intended to establish cordial relations between the two families.

The most essential feature in the wedding is *Mehr* or dower payable by husband to wife – the amount of which is fixed by the representatives of the bride and groom. Whatever the sum, its purpose is to ensure security for the bride.

There are two kinds of *Mehr* – *Moajjal* or immediate, and *Mowajjal* meaning deferred. The latter is more common as the money is payable to the wife if she is divorced or if the husband dies before she does. The *Mehr* is in addition to her share of the deceased's property. The deferred money is payable on demand at any time after the *Nikah* or marriage.

The wedding ceremony lasts for a few minutes and when the *Qadhi* (Muslim Judge) solemnizes the contract of marriage between the bridegroom and the bride, he blesses the marriage with invocations from the *Holy Quran*.

As soon as the *Nikah* ceremony is over, dates are distributed and the prayers for the newly married couple's happiness are offered. Some parts of the prayer translate thus:

'O mankind! Be careful of your duty to your Lord, Who created you from a single soul and from it created its mate and from twain hath spread abroad a multitude of men and women. Be careful of your duty towards Allah in Whom you claim (your rights) of one another, and towards the wombs (that bear). Lo Allah has been a watcher over you' (Al-Qur'an 4:1) *'Marry of the women, who seem good to you'* (Al-Qur'an 4:3) *'Wedlock is my way. He who turns away from my way is not mine,'* the Prophet Muhammad ﷺ said; *'Give women in marriage to men they approve of,'* he added.

Soon after the *Nikah* the bride departs with her husband to her new home. The men of the family, from grandparents to the youngest nephews, gather round the bride and bless her one by one and bid her goodbye. Relations and friends call out *'Khuda-Hafiz'* (Allah Bless). At the groom's house more celebrations take place. These have a twofold purpose, to give thanks and to initiate the bride into her new household. The following day the groom's family hold the *Valeema* – which is a lavish dinner. The wedding is now considered to be over but sporadic ceremonies, designed to integrate the bride into her new family and to symbolize lasting happiness, may continue till after the birth of the first child.

Fatima points out to her English friend that except for some ceremonies like the *Nikah* contract performed by the religious leader, a small dower, and a humble *Valeema*, the other ceremonies are not required according to Islamic traditions.

Fatima's friend is troubled about the idea that Muslim men are allowed to marry up to four wives. Fatima assures her that in the days of the Prophet this was a restrictive number as men then had as many wives as they liked. Moreover, the *Holy Quran* strongly recommends men to be content with one wife as it is impossible to do justice to two or more. Nowadays Muslims usually have only one wife. She laughs to think that Ahmad finds one wife quite sufficient and so do all his friends.

A Birth

On the next occasion when they meet, Fatima is delighted to inform her friend that a cousin is to have her first child. This is always regarded as a special time for both husband and wife. It is the hope of all Muslims to have children, always of course *Inshallah* – Allah willing.

As soon as the child is born the *Adhan* is read into its right ear and a similar prayer in the left. Thus, the first words a Muslim baby hears are those of prayer and devotion to Allah. After some time the baby's head is shaved and a sheep or goat is sacrificed (two for a boy and one for a girl) and the meat is given to the poor. The baby is named after one or two of the 99 names of Allah and those of the Prophet Muhammad ﷺ. The elderly members of the family like to advise in this matter. Sometimes the religious leader opens the *Holy Quran* at random and picks a name from a page. The baby boys are circumcized at an early age, usually by the village barber in the absence of a qualified doctor. Muslim families in Britain retain these religious practices which are often accompanied by a party.

All Muslim families get together on such occasions. For example, Fatima's nephew in Pakistan becomes engaged – and friends come to Ahmad's house to offer their congratulations; Fatima buys sweet meats and entertains visitors with cups of tea and cakes. She expresses her happiness on many different family and communal occasions such as a marriage, a birth, the passing of examinations and job promotions. But a sad occasion for Fatima is the sudden death of a friend.

A Funeral

A Muslim funeral in Great Britain still retains much of the Islamic character and ritual. People who sit with a dying person are recommended to recite the *Kalimah* so that he or she also begins to repeat it with them. At the time of death tears are shed but wailing is forbidden and instead prayers for the dead are encouraged.

The dead body is specially washed and dressed in a loose white unsewn garment made from three or five pieces of sheet for men and women respectively. Immediately after dressing the body it is taken to a local Mosque or the specially allocated graveyard where the *Imam* leads the prayers. The mourners, men only, stand behind him facing the dead body and the *Kaaba*. There is no bending or bowing in funeral prayers. Muslims learn the text which asks for Allah's blessings upon the dead. As the funeral passes by people are expected to stand in respect.

The first level of the grave should be at least two feet deep; and the second level is dug further to make it four feet deep. This should be parallel to the *Kaaba* in Mecca and the body placed with its face towards the *Kaaba*. The second depth is covered with bricks or wooden planks and the rest filled up with earth to make a slight mound. The details of the formulas recited along with the movements are given in the books on Islam. Lavish spending on the construction of the grave is forbidden. A person visiting the grave usually greets the dead saying:

'O, the dwellers of the grave! Peace be upon you. May Allah forgive us all. You went to Him before us and we will follow you.'

For many days after the funeral Muslims read extensively from the *Holy Quran* praying for blessing upon the departed soul. Muslims believe that soon after the burial two angels visit the person for accounts of his wordly deeds and henceforth he lives his real and permanent life, in the life Hereafter.

In the past Muslims in Britain have sent their dead back to Pakistan at exorbitant cost. Now this practice is declining, nevertheless friends and relations do contribute to fly the dead to Pakistan if the need arises.

8   *Islam and Education*

The role of the Mosque in Great Britain is similar to that in Islamic countries. In earlier times, as institutes of learning, they were responsible for the social, cultural, scientific and artistic education of the people. Al-Ghazzali, the great Muslim philosopher and mystic of the twelfth century always had about three hundred students in Baghdad (Iraq) constantly engaged in learning. In the tenth century the Muslims in Spain, known as Moors, gave to the Western world new wisdom and knowledge in agriculture, industry, medicine and architecture. Until 1969 the thousand-year-old Muslim University of Al-Azhar in Cairo (Egypt) mostly admitted students who knew the *Holy Quran* by heart.

Muslims believe that Islam not only teaches about the relationship between man and his Creator but also describes man's superiority over the rest of the worldly creatures. *'Surely we created man in the best of moulds,'* says the *Holy Quran* (95:4). This has helped him to explore nature around him. The five fundamentals of Islam require believers to acquire knowledge in different branches of education in order to carry out their religious beliefs properly. Belief in *Kalimah* requires a certain amount of philosophical study; prayers make men realize the importance of the time and space; fasting gives a greater understanding of natural desires; routes need to be explored and transport selected for pilgrimages; while alms-giving requires some knowledge of mathematics. The study of the *Holy Quran* in its historical context demands a profound knowledge of the Arabic language.

In the early days of Islam these facts were attended to and

a great deal of progress was made in the fields of both art and science.

During the life time of the Prophet Muhammad ﷺ (d. 632 CE) *Salman al-Farsi* (one of the Prophet's companions) translated certain parts of the *Holy Quran* into Persian and this example was followed by other translations of the holy book into almost all languages of the world today. Historians wrote thousands of pages in their biographies of the Prophet, such was the care taken to observe and record his daily life. Later, hundreds of Greek and Sanskrit works were translated into Arabic which are preserved to the present day. Al-Kindi (d. 900), al-Farabi (d. 950), Avicenna (Abu Ibn Sina, d. 1073), Averroes (Ibn Rushid, d. 1198) and others who were well versed in Greek and Indian philosophy brought in new ideas from Greek civilizations and made them Islamic. The Prophet himself governed, and was the author of the first written constitution of the city-state of Medina. Juridical interpretations of the *Holy Quran* and the Prophet's sayings were developed into an Islamic Law which received substantial contributions from the famous jurists Abu Hanaifa (d. 767), Ibn Hanbal (d. 855), Malik (d. 795) and Ash-Shafi (d. 820) who have followers among Muslims all over the world. Ibn Khaldun (d. 1406) wrote a celebrated *Prolegomena to Universal History* which is taught in some British Universities today. The earliest maps prepared by Ibn Hauqal (d. 975) and al-Idrisi (d. 1164) showed a spherical earth with the countries drawn with remarkable precision. During the rule of the Caliph al-Mamun (d. 833) the circumference of the earth was measured and such geographical phenomena as the ebb and flow of the tide, the rainbow, changes of the seasons and other astronomical processes were explained.

Natural sciences such as anatomy, zoology, botany and mineralogy also received the attention of earlier Muslims. The *Encyclopaedia Botanica* of al-Dinawari (d. 895) consisting of six volumes describes the plants, their alimentary and

37

medicinal properties. In the field of optics Ibn al-Haitham (Alhazen, d. 965) developed incendiary mirrors.

Trigonometry was discovered by the well-known Muslim mathematicians Umar al-Khayyam (d. 1131) and al-Biruni (d. 1048). The latter also studied the craft of gem-cutting. Ibn Firnas (d. 921) invented a flying machine and in fact died during a flying expedition. A famous Muslim chemist Jabir Ibn-Hayyan (d. 776) knew the physical processes of evaporation, sublimation and crystallization and the chemical processes of calcination and reduction. He devised the process for the manufacture of sulphuric acid, an essential in the heavy industry of the modern age.

9 *Islamic Brotherhood*

A Muslim lady and her husband have just returned from Saudi Arabia and are now addressed as *Hajin and Haji*. They tell of over two million people of all colours and from all over the world performing the pilgrimage at Mecca. When they meet together at Mecca for their pilgrimage they all wear the same simple clothes so that no one can distinguish between rich and poor. Men and women of all races mix together under the common brotherhood of Islam.

A very devout Afro-American, converted to Islam in prison after leading a life of crime wrote his impressions of the pilgrimage:

> '*During the past eleven days here in the Muslim world, I have eaten from the same plate, drunk from the same glass, and slept in the same bed (or on the same rug). I prayed to the same Allah with fellow Muslims, whose eyes were the bluest of blue, whose hair was the blondest of blond and whose skin was the whitest of white. And in the words and in the actions and in the deeds of white Muslims I felt the same sincerity that I felt among the black Muslims of Nigeria, Sudan, and Ghana. We were truly all the same (brothers) because their belief in one God had removed the "white" from their minds, the "white" from their behaviour, and the "white" from their attitude.*'

These feelings sprang from the heart of a man who lived in a society devoid of human equality and compassion, divided by colour, race and creed and who, after embracing Islam, lived a new life in the Muslim world. In pre-Islamic Arabia the conditions were even worse. Anyone who did not belong to a famous family like the *Quraish*, was considered a slave. The Prophet Muhammad ﷺ, brought the Divine message which proclaimed:

> '*O, Mankind! We created you from a single (pair) of a male and female and made you into nations and tribes that you may know each other (not that you may despise each other). Verily the most honoured of you in the sight of Allah is the most righteous of you.*'
> (*Al-Qur'an 49:13*)

and later remarked:

> '*I affirm that all human beings are brothers unto one another.*'
> '*Respect the ways of Allah and be affectionate to the family of Allah*'

In his famous *Farewell Address* he mentioned that no Arab was superior to a non-Arab except on the grounds of piety which demands the fulfilment of the basic principles of Islam and the practice of such characteristics as kindness, truthfulness, forgiveness, honesty, humility and love for fellow human beings. Thus are obliterated distinctions of race, colour or tribal origin.

Unfortunately, as with the Prophets before him, Muhammad ﷺ and his preaching were not always followed. Muslims, being merely human, soon began to lose sight of the ideals and difficult tasks which Islam requires. It was all too easy to become involved in racial strife and national rivalries. Only the immediate successors of the Prophet Muhammad ﷺ and a certain few of the later Muslim rulers bravely upheld his teaching to the great benefit not only of Muslims but of people of all faiths.

Umar ﷛, the Second Caliph of Islam once received a complaint from an Arab Bedouin who had trodden upon the cloak of the Prince of Ghassan during the rites of pilgrimage and was slapped by the Prince. For this ill-treatment the Caliph ordered that the victim be given the chance to slap the Prince in the way he had been slapped. The Caliph remarked to the Prince, 'Islam made you one with him, and you have no superiority over him except in piety and good works. Rid yourself of the idea that you are a Prince and he a common man.' Umar cautioned him further, 'Since when have you enslaved people who were free, according to Islam?' Wherever the true spirit of Islam has abounded all people have found justice and freedom. But where man's greed has come before his religion then he has sown the seed of his own disaster.

There is today, among concerned and deep-thinking Muslims, a movement to try to recover and practise more vigorously the moral, social and political legislation of the *Holy Quran* and the Prophet's teachings.

Ahmad's own country of Pakistan was set up as an Islamic state. Muslims all over the world are praying that this kind of ideal society can survive in the modern world.

Leading Muslims know that it is only through unity in their religious beliefs that Muslims may once more influence the affairs of the world. With the approach of the fifteenth century of the *Hijra* in 1980, it is hoped that the process of renaissance of Islam, already set in motion in certain Muslim countries, will see its fulfilment in benefit for all mankind.

Look at the charter of the *Universal Declaration of Human Rights*. You will find many which have already been given to humanity by the Holy Prophet Muhammad ﷺ in his sermon delivered at the *Farewell Pilgrimage* fourteen centuries ago:

1. All human beings are born free and equal in dignity and rights.
2. All are equal before the law and are entitled without any discrimination to equal protection of the law.
3. Education shall promote understanding, tolerance and friendship among all nations, racial or religious groups.

And what of the non-rulers of this world, the hundreds and thousands of people who do try to adhere to the main principles of their religion, their way of life? Within their own hearts they too seek these ideals, set out so many years before by Allah, and His Prophet ﷺ.

Next time you see Azra or Ajmal, don't just pass them by, get to know them better, you will probably find that their thoughts are your thoughts and the aspirations of your parents and their parents before them are the same as those of Bashir Ahmad, his wife Fatima and their fellow Muslims throughout the world.

Some Additional Practical Suggestions

Although there is scope for discussion and the introduction of audio-visual aids, anything in the nature of pupils' books could be a supplement to this study. Below are some items which the pupils could include in their books:

> outline map of the Eastern Hemisphere, on which Islamic countries may be shaded in;
> photographs or line drawings illustrating the various positions adopted in the Muslim prayers;
> outline map of Britain, on which major areas in which British Muslims are concentrated may be marked;
> reproduction of photographs of Muslims from different lands, showing characteristic dress;
> some Arabic as illustration of Arabic script;
> a menu for a Muslim restaurant;
> children and teacher may discuss aspects of Islam which are akin to Christianity;
> some key passages from the *Holy Quran* may be written and learnt as poems.

More Ideas

1. Is there a Home Tutor scheme in your district? Contact your Local Community Relations Office and see what you can find out. Some schools help in this work by helping teenage Asians with the English language. Many have made good friends too. You might be able to form a Home Tutor Group in your school.

2. How many religious denominations are there in your class and school? Make a graph of your findings. Try to organize an inter-faith assembly for your class or school.

3. Much of the food eaten by Muslims is different from your own, especially herbs. Find out about these foods. Some have particular medical qualities. What are they? Where can you buy them? What value do cereals and pulse foods play in the Muslim diet? Make lists of cereals and pulse foods used.

Find and draw some oriental vegetables. Can you find some dishes to make using these vegetables?

4. Discuss the value of wearing *shalwar*, from religious and social points of view. How could this fashion be modified?

Appendix A

Prayers

Each service of the prayer consists of two parts – one to be said alone and the other in congregation in the Mosque. When praying alone, both parts are performed. The morning or *Fajr* prayer consists of two individual and two congregational *Rak'ats*. The mid-day or *Zuhr* prayer consists of four individual and then four congregational, followed by two more individual *Rak'ats*. The afternoon or *Asr* prayer consists of four congregational *Rak'ats* while the sunset or *Maghrib* prayer consists of three *Rak'ats* in congregation and two alone. The night or *Isha* prayer consists of four congregational, two individual, three individual *Rak'ats*. Each prayer is timed by a call to prayer. A *Rak'at*, written, said and memorized in Arabic consists of the following steps.

1. *Takbir-i-tahrima:* With the face towards the *Kaaba* in Mecca and in a standing position both hands are raised up to the ears. Simultaneously, اَللهُ اَكْبَرُ or 'Allah is Great' is proclaimed.

2. *Qiyam:* Both hands are folded across the chest while standing; the recitation follows thus:

'*Subhanaka Allahumma-a wa bi hamd-i-ka wa tabarakasmu-ka wa ta'ala Jadd-o-ka wa laila-ha ghair-u-ka.*
Aoozo billa-hi min-ash-Shaitan-ir-rajeem.'

سُبْحٰنَكَ اللّٰهُمَّ وَ بِحَمْدِكَ وَ تَبَارَكَ
اسْمُكَ وَ تَعَالٰى جَدُّكَ وَلَا إِلٰهَ غَيْرُكَ ٥
اَعُوْذُ بِاللهِ مِنَ الشَّيْطٰنِ الرَّجِيْمِ ٥

Glory to thee, O Allah, and Thine is the praise, and blessed is Thy Name and exalted is Thy Majesty, and there is none to be served besides Thee . . . I betake me for refuge to Allah against the accursed Satan.

44

This is followed by the first chapter of the *Holy Quran* i.e. *Al-Fatiha* or *Opening* and any portion of the *Holy Quran* e.g. *Al-Ikhlas*. See Arabic scripts on pages 4 (*Al-Ikhlas*) and 7 (*Al-Fatiha*).

3. *Rukoo*: At the end of *Al-Ikhlas* and saying of *Allah-u-Akbar* the head is lowered while the palms of the hands rest on the knees and *Subhana Rabbiyal Azim!* سُبْحَانَ رَبِّيَ الْعَظِيْمِ ٥ meaning 'Glory to my Lord the Great' is pronounced three times. The person stands erect and utters: *Sami Allahu Leman Hameda Rabbana Lakal Hamd!* سَمِعَ اللهُ لِمَنْ حَمِدَهُ ٥ رَبَّنَا لَكَ الْحَمْدُ ٥ meaning 'Allah accepts him who gives praise to Him; O, our Lord, Thine is the praise.'

4. *Sajdah and Jalsa*: Then the worshipper prostrates himself in a crouched position and with the forehead, nose, palms of both hands, knees and toes of both feet touching the ground and the back partly raised up and says three times *Subhana Rabbiyal Aala!* سُبْحَانَ رَبِّيَ الْأَعْلَى ٥ meaning 'Glory to my Lord the most High.' Then the worshipper sits in a reverential position called *Jalsa*. There follows another *Sajdah* with the three pronouncements as in the first *Sajdah*.

5. *Qa'da*: Towards the end of the second *Sajdah* the worshipper stands up and repeats all points from 2–4 in the second *Rak'at* of the prayer. This time at the end of the second *Rak'at* he stays sitting in a reverential position called *Qa'da* with the palms on the knees and recites the following:

'*At tahiyy at-u-lillah-i-was salawat-u way-tay yebat-u, As-Salam-u, alaika Ayyuhan-nabiyyu wa rahmat ullah-i wa bara katuh As-Salam-u alaina Wal ala' ibad-illah-is salihin. Ash-hadu al-la ilaha illallah wa ash-hadu anna Mauammadan abdu-hu wa rasulu-hu.*'

اَلتَّحِيَّاتُ لِلهِ وَ الصَّلَوَاتُ وَ الطَّيِّبَاتُ اَلسَّلَامُ عَلَيْكَ اَيُّهَا النَّبِيُّ وَ رَحْمَةُ اللهِ وَ بَرَكَاتُهُ اَلسَّلَامُ عَلَيْنَا وَ عَلَى عِبَادِ اللهِ الصَّالِحِيْنَ ٠ اَشْهَدُ اَنْ لَّا اِلٰهَ اِلَّا اللهُ وَ اَشْهَدُ اَنَّ مُحَمَّدًا عَبْدُهُ وَ رَسُوْلُهُ

'All prayer and worship rendered through words, actions, and wealth are due to Allah. Peace be on you O Prophet and the mercy of Allah and His Blessings. Peace be on us and the righteous servants of Allah. And I bear witness that Muhammad is His servant and His Apostle.'

If this is the second *Rak'at* of the four the worshipper stands up again and repeats the steps 2–4 for the third *Rak'at* and stands up and repeats the steps 2–5 and adds the following prayer of blessings for the Prophet at the end of the fifth step.

'Allah-humma salli ala Muhammad-in wa'ala ali Muhammad-in kama sallaita 'ala Ibrahima wa 'ala a'li Ibrahima, inna-ka hamid-um majid. Allah humma barik 'ala Muhammad-in wa'ala ali Muhammad-in Kama barakta 'ala Ibrahima wa'ala a'li Ibrahima inna-ka hamid-un majid.'

اَللّٰهُمَّ صَلِّ عَلٰى مُحَمَّدٍ وَّ عَلٰى
اٰلِ مُحَمَّدٍ كَمَا صَلَّيْتَ عَلٰى اِبْرَاهِيْمَ وَ عَلٰى
اٰلِ اِبْرَاهِيْمَ اِنَّكَ حَمِيْدٌ مَّجِيْدٌ ٥ اَللّٰهُمَّ
بَارِكْ عَلٰى مُحَمَّدٍ وَّ عَلٰى اٰلِ مُحَمَّدٍ
كَمَا بَارَكْتَ عَلٰى اِبْرَاهِيْمَ وَ عَلٰى اٰلِ اِبْرَاهِيْمَ
اِنَّكَ حَمِيْدٌ مَّجِيْدٌ ٥

'O Allah magnify Muhammad and the followers of Muhammad as thou didst magnify Abraham and the followers of Abraham, for surely Thou art praised and magnified. O Allah! bless Muhammad and the followers of Muhammad as Thou didst bless Abraham and the followers of Abraham for surely Thou are blessed and magnified.'

The following may be added:

'Rabbij alni muqim-as-salat-i wa min zurriyati Rabbana wa taqabbal du'a Rabbana – aghfir-li wa li-wali-dayya wa-lil mum-inina yauma yaqumul his-ab.'

رَبِّ اجْعَلْنِيْ مُقِيْمَ الصَّلٰوةِ وَ مِنْ ذُرِّيَّتِيْ
رَبَّنَا وَ تَقَبَّلْ دُعَآءِ ٥ رَبَّنَا اغْفِرْلِيْ وَ
لِوَالِدَيَّ وَ لِلْمُؤْمِنِيْنَ يَوْمَ يَقُوْمُ الْحِسَابُ ٥

'My Lord! make me to keep up prayer and my offsprings too;
Our Lord! accept the prayer; Our Lord! Thy protection to me
and my parents and to the faithful on the day when the
reckoning shall be taken.'

6. *Salam:* Then the worshipper turns his head first to the
right and then to the left saying each time *Assalamu Alaikum Wa Rahmatullah!* ٥ السَّلَامُ عَلَيْكُمْ وَ رَحْمَةُ اللهِ meaning
'peace be with you and the mercy of Allah'. In the night or
Isha prayer, during *Witr,* the third Rak'at is performed
exactly the same way as the fourth except that after arising
from the last *Rukoo,* and while still standing, the worshipper pronounces the additional prayer.

'*Allah umma inna nasta'inuka wa nastaghfiruka wa numina bi-
ka wa natawakkalu 'alaika wa nusni 'alaikal khair wa nash-
kuru-ka wa la nakfuru-ka wa nakhla'-o wa natruku man yaf-
juru-ka Allahumma iyyaka nabud-u wa laka nussali wa nusjudu
wa ilaika nasaa wa Nahfidu wa narju rahmataka wa nakhsha
azabaka inna 'azaabaka bil kuffari mulhiq.*'

اَللَّهُمَّ اِنَّا نَسْتَعِيْنُكَ وَ نَسْتَغْفِرُكَ
وَ نُؤْمِنُ بِكَ وَ نَتَوَكَّلُ عَلَيْكَ وَ نُثْنِيْ
عَلَيْكَ الْخَيْرَ وَ نَشْكُرُكَ وَ لَا نَكْفُرُكَ
وَ نَخْلَعُ وَ نَتْرُكُ مَنْ يَفْجُرُكَ ٥ اَللَّهُمَّ
اِيَّاكَ نَعْبُدُ وَ لَكَ نُصَلِّي وَ نَسْجُدُ
وَ اِلَيْكَ نَسْعَى وَ نَخْفِدُ وَ نَرْجُوْ رَحْمَتَكَ
وَ نَخْشَى عَذَابَكَ اِنَّ عَذَابَكَ بِالْكُفَّارِ مُلْحِقٌ ٥

'O Allah! we beseech Thy help. And ask Thy protection and
believe in Thee and trust on Thee, and we laud Thee in the
best manner and we thank Thee, and we cast off and forsake
him who disobeys Thee! O Allah! Thee do we serve and to
Thee do we pray and make obeisance, and to Thee do we fly,
and we are quick and we hope for Thy mercy and we fear Thy
punishment, for surely Thy punishment overtakes the un-
believer.'

Du'a (supplication) after completing Farz Rak'at:
*Rabbana! La Toaakhizna inna sinā au akhtana. Rabbana! Wa
la Tahmil 'alaina isran kama hamaltahu 'alallazina min qab-
lina. Rabbana! Wa la tohammilna ma la taqata lana bihee.*

*Wa'fu 'anna, waghfirlana, warhamna, anta maulana fansurna
'alal qaum-il-kāfirin.*

رَبَّنَا لَا تُؤَاخِذْنَا إِنْ نَسِينَا أَوْ أَخْطَأْنَا ۚ
رَبَّنَا وَ لَا تَحْمِلْ عَلَيْنَا إِصْرًا كَمَا حَمَلْتَهُ
عَلَى الَّذِينَ مِنْ قَبْلِنَا ۚ رَبَّنَا وَ لَا تُحَمِّلْنَا
مَا لَا طَاقَةَ لَنَا بِهِ ۖ وَاعْفُ عَنَّا ۗ وَ اغْفِرْ لَنَا ۗ
وَارْحَمْنَا ۚ أَنْتَ مَوْلَانَا فَانْصُرْنَا عَلَى الْقَوْمِ الْكَافِرِينَ ۝

'Our Lord!
Condemn us not
If we forget or fall
Into error; our Lord!
Lay not on us a burden
Like that which Thou
Didst lay on those before us;
Our Lord! lay not on us
A burden greater than we
Have strength to bear.
Blot out our sins,
And grant us forgiveness.
Have mercy on us.
Thou art our Protector;
Help us against those
Who stand against Faith,'
          —*(Abdullah Yusuf Ali translation — Al-Qur'an 2:286)*

Appendix D

Glossary of Arabic Terms

Some of the Arabic/Urdu theological terms which a reader may come across, in the suggested books are translated for easy reading.

Abbasid, Ummayed, Rashidin and Ottoman: these are the names of the Muslim Caliphates in a chronological order beginning in 632 CE with Rashidin and ending with Ottoman in 1932 CE.

Akhira: Life after death.

Alim: See *Ulama* below.

Allah: Allah is the Arabic proper name for God, the Omnipotent, the Unique, the One and the Only Lord, the Master, the Creator, the Sustainer and the Destroyer.

Amir-ul-Mumineen: The Commander of the Faithful (Ruler of the Muslims).

Ansar: Helper – Title given to all those residents of Medina who helped the Muslims who migrated from Mecca along with the Prophet, peace be upon him, and immediately after him.

Ashrafi: Name of a gold coin used in Iraq.

Assalam-u-Alaikum! Peace be on you (a common greeting among the Muslims).

Bait-ul-Maqdis: The olden name of Al-Aqsa Mosque in Jerusalem (Palestine).

Bin: Son of, e.g. Zaid bin Hartha, meaning Zaid son of Hartha.

Bismillah-irrahman-irrahim: Means 'In the Name of Allah, the Most Compassionate, the Most Merciful.' Every Muslim remembers this formula by heart and utters it at the beginning of all daily jobs.

Caliphate: Succession/rule.

Caliph/Khalifa in Arabic: Successor/leader.

Dawood: The Prophet David, peace be on him.

Dirham: Name of a gold coin used in Persia/Iran.

Dua: Supplication.

Fiqh: Jurisprudence.

Hadith: Sayings, actions or approvals of the Prophet Muhammad ﷺ, peace and blessings of Allah the Almighty be on him.

Halal: That which is lawful, i.e. permitted in Islamic Law (*Shari'a*).

Hajj: Effort – one of the fundamentals of Islam; pilgrimage to Mecca and Medina in Saudi Arabia.

Haram: That which is unlawful, i.e. forbidden in the Islamic Law.

Hijrah: Emigration of the Prophet Muhammad ﷺ from Mecca to Medina at the Command from Allah the Almighty. This was the 16th July 622 CE and marks the beginning of the Islamic Calendar.

Huquq-Allah: Rights of Allah the Almighty over men and women: man's obligations and duties towards Allah the Almighty.

Huquq ul-Ibad: Rights of men over men: Men's obligations and duties towards Allah the Almighty's creatures.

Ibrahim: The Prophet Abraham, peace be upon him.

Imam: A leader, a guide, an example, a model of the Muslims in a Mosque, town or country.

Innalillahi wa inna Ilaihi Rajiun: Means 'all of us came from Allah and we will all return to Allah the Almighty.' A Muslim recites it instantaneously at the news of a death.

Isa: The Prophet Jesus, peace be upon him.

Islam: Islam, the Religion of about 900,000,000 Muslims all over the world, has two literal meanings, 'submission to the Will of Allah the Almighty' and 'peace'.

Jihad: Struggle in the path of Allah the Almighty.

Jinn: Genii.

Juz: One part of the *Holy Quran* which is divided into 30 *juz* or parts.

Kaaba: A cube-shaped building which is situated in Mecca and is a place of worship for Muslims. Muslims throughout the world turn their faces in the direction of the *Kaaba* in their daily prayers. The first *Kaaba* of the Muslims was Al-Aqsa in Palestine.

Kalimah: Tenet of the Muslim Faith, i.e. there is no deity but

Allah (the Almighty) and Muhammad (peace be upon him) is the Messenger of Allah (the Almighty).

Kalimahs: There are four other *Kalimahs* meaning 'euphorisms' besides the one relating to the Faith.

Khalifa: Caliph.

Khalifa-tul-Lah: Vicegerent of Allah the Almighty, i.e. man.

Khanqah: A place where Muslim men and women lead a life of devotion to Allah the Almighty.

Khulaf-ar-Rashidoon: The purified Caliphs, a term generally used to mean the first Four Caliphs of Islam; Hazrat Abu Bakr, Hazrat Umar, Hazrat Uthman, and Hazrat Ali, may Allah the Almighty be pleased with them all.

Lota: An Urdu word used for a round earthen or metallic vessel of 3–4 pints capacity used for ablutions at home or for toilet.

Madrassah: School.

Maryam: The Arabic name for Mary, the mother of Jesus. This is a common name among Muslim ladies all over the world.

Miraj: Ascension to Heaven of the Prophet Muhammad صلى الله عليه وسلم, peace be upon him, during a part of the night in the 27th Rajab (7th month of the lunar calendar) and his journey to Jerusalem and later through the Heavens.

Mosque: The place of worship for Muslims.

Muhajirun: Migrants – A title which was given to the Companions of the Prophet, peace be upon him, who accompanied him in the *Hijrah.*

Muhammad (Sallallah-u Alaihi Wasallam): The Prophet Muhammad صلى الله عليه وسلم.

Mujaddid: One who revives religious fervour and idealism.

Musa: The Prophet Moses, peace be upon him.

Muslim: The one who submits to the Will of Allah the Almighty – the follower of Islam.

Qibla: Direction of prayers towards the *Kaaba* in Mecca.

Qunut: The invocation which is recited in the last night prayer.

Quraish: A noble Arab Meccan tribe to which the Prophet Muhammad صلى الله عليه وسلم belonged.

Quran: The true revealed word of Allah the Almighty meaning 'recitation' – the religious *Holy Book* of the Muslims.

Ramadhan: The name of the 9th month of fasting of the lunar calendar.

Risalat: Institution of Prophets, peace be on them all.

Salat: Prayers five times a day.

Saum: Fasting during the month of *Ramadhan.*

Shari'a: The Islamic Law, literally meaning the 'path'.

Sufi: One who wears clothes made of *suf* (wool), usually the pious people; Muslim mystics.

Sulaiman: The Prophet Solomon, peace be upon him.

Sunnah: Same as *Hadith.*

Sura: A chapter of the *Holy Quran.*

Syedena: Our leader.

Tafsir: Exegesis.

Tauheed: Unity of Allah and Science of Islamic Theology.

Tariqah: Muslim mystical path.

Tasawwuf: Islamic Mysticism.

Tawakkal: Contentment with one's lot.

Ulama: The learned scholar in Islam (singular – *Alim*).

Wa Alaikum Salam: And peace be upon you – an answer to the greeting *Asaalam-u-Alaikum.*

Wudhu: Ablution (performed before each prayer).

Yusuf: The Prophet Joseph, peace be upon him.

Zakat: Almsgiving which is compulsory on every Muslim who has wealth or property.

Help from any Arab, or Asian Muslim, in pronouncing the above Arabic terms would be invaluable to any one unfamiliar with the language. Some terms have long explanations because of the lack of a one-word English equivalent just as some English words have no one word equivalent in Arabic.